THE COLLECTED
FAT FREDDY'S
CAT

VOLUME TWO

D1710048

BY GILBERT SHELTON

WITH DAVE SHERIDAN

3

FREEWHEELIN' FRANKLIN WON'T MIND IF I BORROW HIS TYPEWRITER FOR A COUPLE OF DAYS TO KNOCK OUT MY SCREENPLAY!

IN MY MOVIE THERE WILL BE BIRDS, RATS, DOGS, RACOONS, HAMSTERS, PIGS, GOLDFISH, GERBILS, PARAKEETS AND CATS!

...BUT MAINLY CATS!

AND YOU, MY FURRY FRIEND, ARE GOING TO BE THE NEXT BIG ANIMAL SUPERSTAR, AND I, FAT FREDDY, WILL BE YOUR MANAGER!

A SHORT TIME LATER, A BATTERED VOLKSWAGEN VAN PULLS INTO THE MOVIE CAPITAL OF THE WORLD.

HERE IT IS, PUSSYCAT! HOLLYWOOD!

WILL YOU PLEASE STOP BITING AND SCRATCHING ME?

MEGALITHIC MOVIES INC.

THIS LOOKS LIKE AS GOOD A PLACE AS ANY TO DO IT!

I'M SORRY, MR. FREEKOWTSKI, BUT MEGALITHIC JUST ISN'T INTERESTED IN READING YOUR SCREENPLAY "DISCO KITTY MEETS THE MEOWBEASTS OF MARS!"

BUT... BUT YOU HAVEN'T EVEN SEEN MY CAT YET!

DESPITE HIS ELOQUENT PLEAS, FAT FREDDY IS POLITELY ESCORTED FROM EVERY MOTION PICTURE STUDIO IN HOLLYWOOD, ONE BY ONE.

YOU FOOLS! YOU'RE PASSING UP THE IDEA OF THE DECADE!

SPACE DOGFIGHTS WITH REAL DOGS! THAT'LL GET THE SCIENCE-FICTION CROWD IN THERE WITH THE DOG AUDIENCE! LOOK! WE'LL HAVE FLIPPER AND LASSIE IN IT IN CAMEO ROLES! IS LASSIE STILL ALIVE?

...AND THE STAR OF THE SHOW IS THAT HOT LITTLE PROPERTY OF MINE, THIS CAT HERE... HE'S A DANCING CAT, DOES THE TANGO, THE FANDANGO, YOU NAME IT!!

THE DISCO CROWD, THE FRED ASTAIRE FANS... EVERYONE WILL BE STANDING IN LINE TO SEE IT TIME AFTER TIME! WE CAN'T LOSE! IT'S A NATURAL!!

NOW SHOWING ONE BY FREEKOW...

75th BIG WEEK DISCO KITTY AND THE MEOWBEASTS FROM MARS DIRECTED BY FREDERICK FREEKOW...

ALL SEATS $5.00

THEN...

...AND THE ACADEMY AWARD FOR BEST DIRECTOR-SCREENWRITER FOR THE YEAR 1978...

FREDERICK FREEKOWTSKI!

CLAP HOLLER

CLAP CLAP
CLAP
YELL SCREEAM
CLAP YELL
CLAP SHOUT
CLAP

YOU'LL NEVER TAKE ME ALIVE, FAT FREDDY!

SPROINK

POP

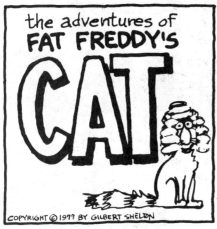

11

the adventures of FAT-FREDDY'S CAT

IN: The Sacred Sands of POOTWEET ...or, The Mayor's Meowter

SOME YEARS AGO, A CLEVER YOUNG LAD, **DICK WHITTINGTON**, WAS OFFERED THE CHANCE OF INCLUDING ARTICLES OF HIS OWN ON ONE OF HIS EMPLOYER'S SHIPS GOING ON AN ASIAN VOYAGE. THIS WAS A SPECIAL PRIVILEGE, A RARE OPPORTUNITY FOR A COMMON SERVANT TO EARN MONEY IN THE EXOTIC OVERSEAS TRADE. DICK WHITTINGTON'S ONLY TRADEABLE POSSESSION, THO', WAS HIS **CAT**.

...AFTER A LONG SEA VOYAGE, **DICK WHITTINGTON'S CAT** ARRIVED IN A COUNTRY WHICH WAS BEING TORMENTED BY A PLAGUE OF **MICE**...

THE GRAND YUHU WAS **VERY** GRATEFUL.

THUSLY, WITH THE AID OF HIS LOYAL **CAT**, DICK WHITTINGTON BEGAN TO AMASS THE **HUGE FORTUNE** WHICH EVENTUALLY ENABLED HIM TO BECOME **LORD MAYOR OF LONDON**.

DID I EVER TELL YOU ABOUT THE TIME OLD **FAT FREDDY** AND I HAD A **SIMILAR** EXPERIENCE?

NOOOOO...

I DON'T THINK SOOOO...

19

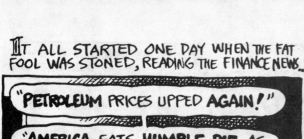

IT ALL STARTED ONE DAY WHEN THE FAT FOOL WAS STONED, READING THE FINANCE NEWS...

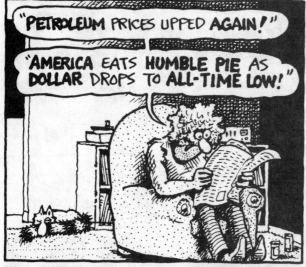

"PETROLEUM PRICES UPPED AGAIN!"

"AMERICA EATS HUMBLE PIE AS DOLLAR DROPS TO ALL-TIME LOW!"

THERE MUST BE SOME WAY WE CAN EVEN OUT THAT MASSIVE IMBALANCE OF PAYMENTS WITH THE OIL NATIONS!

SURELY WE HAVE SOMETHING THAT WE COULD SELL THEM!

HMMMMMMMMM...

IF I REMEMBER CORRECTLY, DICK WHITTINGTON MADE HIS FORTUNE BY SELLING HIS CAT TO THE KING OF SOME PLACE THAT WAS OVERRUN BY MICE! MAYBE I COULD ACTUALLY PULL THE SAME SCAM!

FIRST I'LL NEED SOME MICE!

I'D LIKE A NICE PAIR OF BREEDERS!

MISTER, THEY'RE ALL BREEDERS!

BIRDS

MICE

TURTLES

FISH

A FEW WEEKS LATER:

MOUSE FEED IS COSTING ME FIFTY DOLLARS A DAY NOW! IT'S TIME TO MAKE MY MOVE!

SHORTLY THEREAFTER, FAT FREDDY IS BOUND FOR THE TINY BUT OIL-RICH NATION OF POOTWEET.

A ROUND-TRIP TICKET TO POOTWEET CITY, PLEASE! I'LL CARRY THESE WITH ME, AND THAT GOES IN THE BAGGAGE!

AIR POOTWEE

21

25

IT MAY BE "ONLY KITTY POOP" TO **YOU**, ATHEIST SWINE, BUT TO US **POOTWEETIANS** IT SIGNALS THE BEGINNING OF THE DREADED **PLAGUE** OF **CAT FECES** AS PREDICTED HERE IN THE **EPISTLE** OF THE APOSTLE **PODDY!**

THAT'S ONE OF THE CHAPTERS OF OUR **HOLY GOBBLDYBOOK!**

IT IS WRITTEN:

...and it shall come to pass that the **sacred** sands shall be defiled by the malodorous offal of the common feline, and this shall be a signal to the omnipotent Yawahootie to send a mighty rain of heavenly cat-caca down upon the miserable nation of Pootweet, and this rain shall last thirty-three fortnights, and shall not cease until the inhabitants have all perished, and the very name of Pootweet will cause disgust and a stinging of the nostrils of whomever shall hear it pronounced, forever forth.

THE ENTIRE HISTORY OF THE POOTWEETIAN PEOPLE HAS BEEN THE STRUGGLE TO KEEP ALL THE **CATS** OUT OF THE **SACRED SANDS!**

FORMERLY, HUGE ARMIES OF PEOPLE STOOD GUARD!

ONLY **RECENTLY**, WITH THE HELP OF **MODERN SCIENCE** AND **PETRODOLLARS**, HAVE WE BEEN ABLE DEVELOP OUR TECHNOLOGY OF **CAT COMMODES!** OUR ENTIRE GROSS NATIONAL EFFORT HAS BEEN DEVOTED TO TRAINING THE CREATURES TO USE THE LITTLE TOILETS!

...AND NOW, **ALL IS LOST!** WHEN THEY SEE **YOUR** CAT USING THE SAND, THEY'LL **ALL** WANT TO USE IT!!

JUST A MINUTE! IT'S NOT TOO LATE YET! GIVE ME YOUR **HAT!**

BUT... BUT WE ARE NOT ALLOWED TO **REMOVE** OUR HATS!

THE **CAT** IS **RUNNING BACK!** WHAT **IS** THIS WONDROUS SUBSTANCE?

JUST ASK FOR **POOTER POWDER**, © ™ THE CATBOX FILLER OF THE DISCRIMINATING CONSUMER!

SEE? THEY ACTUALLY **PREFER** IT TO SAND!

IT IS A **MIRACLE!** YAWAHOOTIE BE PRAISED!

DO YOU HAVE ANY OF IT FOR **SALE?** I'D LIKE TO **BUY** SEVERAL HUNDRED BAGS!

(SIGH!)

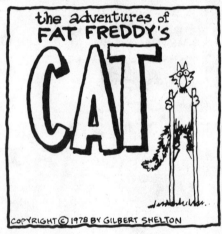

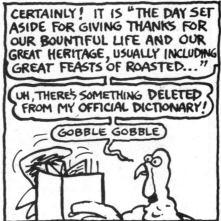

I JUST **LOVE** THAT SHIT-KICKIN MUSIC!

END

the adventures of FAT FREDDY'S CAT

COPYRIGHT © 1980 BY GILBERT SHELTON

THERE'S AN ARTICLE IN THIS WEEK'S **EARTHCHRONICLE** THAT MIGHT BE OF SOME INTEREST TO YOU, FAT FREDDY!

"AMERICANS GONE PET CRAZY," SAYS THE HEADLINE!

IT SAYS THE AVERAGE AMERICAN SPENDS ENOUGH EACH WEEK ON **PET FOOD** TO FEED AN ENTIRE FAMILY IN **CAMBODIA**!

DOESN'T THAT MAKE YOU FEEL **ASHAMED** OF YOURSELF?

NO, BECAUSE I'M **SURE** A FAMILY OF **CAMBODIANS** WOULDN'T MAKE **NEAR** AS GOOD A **PET**!

THAT'S TELLIN' 'EM, FAT FREDDY!

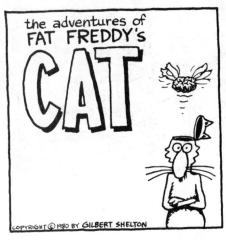

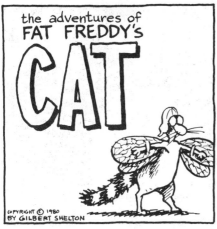

COCKROACH *FACTS*

by GILBERT SHELTON

There are thousands of species of cockroaches, including tropical forest & semiaquatic varieties, woodborers, underground dwellers and species that are parasitic on other insects. Fortunately, only a few are house pests. The four types most commonly encountered are the **American** Cockroach (*Periplaneta americana*), the German Cockroach (*Blattella germanica*), the Oriental Cockroach (*Blatta orientalis*), and the Brown-Banded Cockroach (*Supella longipalpa*). Of these, the largest is the *Periplaneta americana*, a prime specimen of which can be up to two inches long. All of these species came originally from the old world, perhaps Africa. In the summer of 1979, over a million German cockroaches were found in a house in Schenectady, New York. Since then, this city has been known as the **Cockroach Capital of the World.**

Foreign words for cockroach:

German: *Küchenschabe*
French: *blatte* or *cafard*
Spanish: *cucaracha*
Italian: *blatta*
Russian: *tarakán*
Dutch: *kakkerlak*
Chinese: *chang·lang*
Portuguese: *bicho de·conta*
Danish: *kakerlak*
Norwegian: *kakerlakk*
Swedish: *mort*
Polish: *karaluch*
Japanese: *abula mushi*
Hebrew: *juke*

Phyllodromia germanica
(German Cockroach)

Supella longipalpa
(Brown-banded Cockroach)

The cockroach picks up vibrations with its antennae in the front and the **cerci** in the rear, which are attached directly to its legs, avoiding the need for its sensations to be processed by the brain before the legs start in motion. Roaches eat almost anything, a thin layer of grease being enough to keep them happy. They will eat bread, fruit, crackers, grease, sweets, vegetables, pet food, garbage, beer, marijuana, tobacco, cereal, paper, soap, glue, fingernails, toenails, pus, urine, feces, and each other. They produce an unpleasant odor called "attar of roaches," which is the combined product of their excrement, of fluid exuded from their abdominal scent glands and of a dark-colored fluid regurgitated from their mouths while feeding.

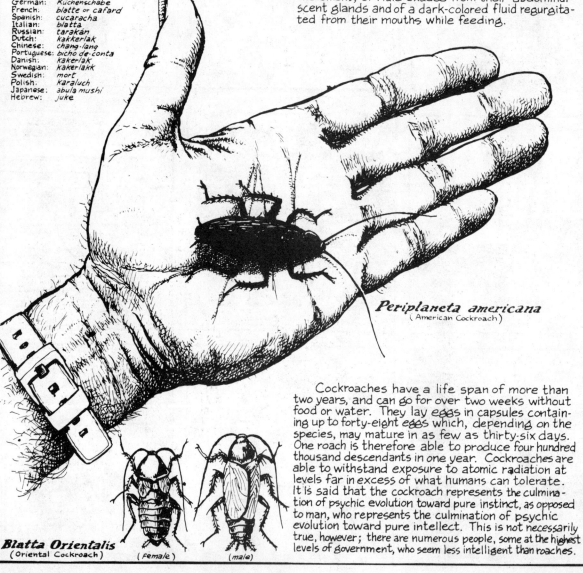

Periplaneta americana
(American Cockroach)

Blatta Orientalis
(Oriental Cockroach)
(female)　(male)

Cockroaches have a life span of more than two years, and can go for over two weeks without food or water. They lay eggs in capsules containing up to forty-eight eggs which, depending on the species, may mature in as few as thirty-six days. One roach is therefore able to produce four hundred thousand descendants in one year. Cockroaches are able to withstand exposure to atomic radiation at levels far in excess of what humans can tolerate. It is said that the cockroach represents the culmination of psychic evolution toward pure instinct, as opposed to man, who represents the culmination of psychic evolution toward pure intellect. This is not necessarily true, however; there are numerous people, some at the highest levels of government, who seem less intelligent than roaches.

A BUNCH OF CATS WERE SITTING AROUND THE GARBAGE CANS ONE DAY TELLING STORIES.

ANY OF YOU EVER GET **LOCKED INSIDE** THE HOUSE OF YOUR "OWNERS"?

YEAH, ONE TIME MINE LOCKED ME IN FOR **TWELVE HOURS!**

BOY, WERE **THEY** SORRY! I REALLY MADE A **MESS** OF THE PLACE!

ONE TIME **MY** HUMANS WENT OFF AND LEFT ME LOCKED INSIDE THE HOUSE FOR A **WHOLE WEEKEND!**

I THINK THEY WENT ALL THE WAY TO THE **OTHER SIDE** OF THE **STATE!**

THEY HAD TO **MOVE** AFTER THAT!

ONCE, **MINE** WENT OFF TO **SOUTH AMERICA!**

50

I WAS IN **PARADISE!**

NOT A SINGLE **HUMAN BEING** TO **TORMENT** AND **ABUSE** ME...

... I COULD **SLEEP** UP ON TOP OF THE **STOVE** WHERE IT WAS **WARM,** FOR INSTANCE...

THERE WAS **FURNITURE** TO TEAR UP, THINGS TO **TURN OVER,** SACKS OF **GARBAGE** TO STREW ABOUT— A **THOUSAND** THINGS FOR A CAT TO DO!

RIP TEAR POP

THERE WAS A TREMENDOUS SACK OF **DRIED CAT FOOD** IN THE **PANTRY** AND **RUNNING WATER** IN THE **TOILET!** I WAS **SET UP** FOR A **LONG TIME!**

PEANUT BUTTER TEA

EKONOMY **KITTY KUBES**

DRY **CAT FOOD**

IT WAS THE **NEIGHBORS** THAT CAUSED ALL THE **PROBLEMS!**

THE NEIGHBORS?

SHORTLY AFTER THE **FREAK BROTHERS** HAD LEFT FOR **BOGOTA,** THERE HAPPENED TO BE A **MEETING** OF THE **TENANTS** OF THE **BUILDING!**

IS EVERYONE HERE?

EVERYBODY EXCEPT THE GUYS IN 2B!

DON'T THEY KNOW ABOUT THE MEETING?

52

I'VE **PHONED** THE LANDLORD **GOD KNOWS HOW** MANY **TIMES** AND ALL I EVER GET IS HIS **ANSWERING MACHINE!** HE'S **NEVER** RETURNED ANY OF MY **CALLS!** NOT **ONE!**

THE **LANDLORD** HASN'T HAD **ANYTHING** REPAIRED IN THIS BUILDING FOR **YEARS!**

I THINK WE CAN SAFELY SAY THE **LANDLORD** IS **NOT** GOING TO BE OF ANY **HELP!**

WE CAN TAKE UP A **COLLECTION** TO HAVE A **PEST CONTROL** SPRAY!

THAT'S EXPENSIVE AS HELL! WE CAN **RENT** A MACHINE AND DO IT **OURSELVES!**

SO JULIUS AND MARVIN RENTED A SPRAYER.

THEY SPRAYED EVERY APARTMENT THOROUGHLY, EXCEPT THE FREAK BROTHERS' WHICH WAS LOCKED.

THEY TRIED TO SQUIRT THE SPRAY UNDER THE DOOR, BUT ONLY A SMALL AMOUNT GOT IN. AFTER A BIT, THEY GAVE UP AND WENT AWAY.

WHEN THE NEIGHBORS WERE ABLE TO RE-ENTER THEIR APARTMENTS, THEY WERE PLEASANTLY SHOCKED.

THE **COCKROACHES** ARE **ALL GONE!**

I DON'T EVEN SEE ANY **DEAD** ONES!

THEY HAD ALL COME INTO **OUR** APARTMENT.

APARTMENT **2B**, BEING IN THE **CENTER** OF THE BUILDING AND THE ONLY PLACE **FREE** OF **POISON**, WAS **INVADED** FROM **ALL SIDES.**

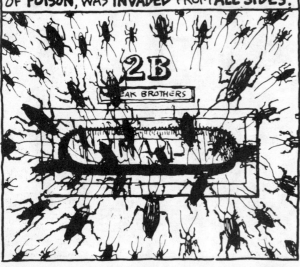

NOW, SINCE 2B WAS THE **DIRTIEST** APARTMENT OF **ALL**, IT NATURALLY HAD AN **INDIGENOUS** COCKROACH POPULATION **ALREADY...**

THERE WERE, IN FACT, TWO LARGE CULTURES: THE **CAPITALIST** COCKROACHES, WHICH LIVED IN THE FECUND AND RESOURCE-RICH **KITCHEN...**

...AND THE **COMMUNIST** COCKROACHES, WHICH INHABITED THE VAST BUT RELATIVELY BARREN REGIONS OF THE **LIVING ROOM** AND **BATHROOM.**

THE **LEADER** OF THE **CAPITALIST** ROACHES WAS AN OLD DEMAGOGUE OF A *BLATTELLA GERMANICA* KNOWN AS **PRESIDENT-COMMANDER-POPE SWELLGUY 3d.**

HE WAS BACKED BY A CADRE OF LOYAL MERCENARY *PERIPLANETAE AMERICANAE* WHO SURROUNDED HIS ROYAL BUNKER UNDERNEATH THE KITCHEN STOVE.

THOUGH OUTNUMBERED BY THE COMMUNIST ROACHES, THE CAPITALISTS' SUPERIOR RESOURCES AND TECHNOLOGY HAD ENABLED THEM TO LIVE IN SECURE ISOLATION.

A RICH HARVEST OF UNCARRIED-OUT GARBAGE WAS THEIRS FOR THE PICKING, AND A WEALTH OF UNWASHED DISHES FILLED THE SINK TO OVERFLOWING.

THE CHIEF PROBLEM THAT HAD FACED THE COCKROACH COLONY OF THE KITCHEN, THEN, IN THE ABSENCE OF ANY DIRECT ATTACKS BY THE DISTANT COMMUNISTS, WAS **BOREDOM.**

BURP.

BURP.

BURP.

THE CAPITALISTS MAINTAINED THEIR MORALE BY HOLDING **MOONLIGHT PEP RALLIES** ON THE BROAD EXPANSE OF LINOLEUM IN FRONT OF THE STOVE.

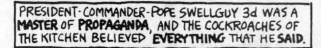

PRESIDENT-COMMANDER-POPE SWELLGUY 3d WAS A **MASTER** OF **PROPAGANDA**, AND THE COCKROACHES OF THE KITCHEN BELIEVED **EVERYTHING** THAT HE **SAID**.

IT HAS BEEN POINTED OUT TO ME BY MY **MILITARY** ADVISORS THAT OUR **MORTAL FOES**, THE **EVIL COMMUNISTS** HAVE DEVELOPED A **NEW BIOLOGICAL WEAPON** TO BE USED AGAINST US: **WINGED PIGS** WHICH ARE CAPABLE OF **FLIGHT!**

AIEEEE! AIEEEE! AIEEE! AIEEEE!

THEREFORE, IN ORDER TO **PROTECT** OUR **GREAT MORAL CIVILIZATION**, WE MUST GATHER **ADDITIONAL FUNDS** FOR OUR **NOBLE FRIENDS** AND **PROTECTORS**, THE **DEFENSE CONTRACTORS** AND THE **BRAVE MEMBERS** OF THE **MILITARY!**

HOORAY! HOORAY! CLAP CLAP CLAP CLAP CLAP CLAP CLAP CLAP

TO DO THIS, I MUST AGAIN **RAISE** THE **TAXES** OF THE **LOWER BRACKETS**, ALTHOUGH I AM SURE THESE CITIZENS WILL NOT **MIND**, SINCE THEY ARE STILL AT LEAST **TWELVE POINT THREE** TIMES BETTER OFF THAN THEIR COMMUNIST COUNTERPART, THOSE MISERABLE, WRETCHED, UNSTYLISHLY-DRESSED WORKERS SUFFERING UNDER THE **GODLESS YOKE!**

12.3 OFFICIAL NUMBER

FALL IN! FORWARD MARCH! PRESENT ARMS! PRESENT LEGS!

ZEKE! HI-Y'ALL! ZEKE! HI-Y'ALL!

STANDIN' TALL! STANDIN' TALL!

*"PRESIDENT-COMMANDER-POPE SWELLGUY 3d's FIRST NAME WAS "ZEKE".

ALL RIGHT, PARADE TIME OVER! NOW, EVERYBODY ON THEIR KNEES FOR **FIVE MINUTES** OF **OFFICIAL VOLUNTARY PRAYER!**

OUR **FODDER**, WHICH ART IN **OVEN** ...

THE KITCHEN ROACHES **OBEYED** SWELLGUY **HAPPILY**.

THE **COMMUNIST** ROACHES WERE LED BY A CRAFTY AND RUTHLESS *BLATTELLA ORIENTALIS* KNOWN AS **PREMIER ATTAR KAKAVICH TARAKAN**.

ATTAR TARAKAN WAS **LIKEWISE** A MASTER OF RHETORIC AND DOGMA, USING HIS TALENTS TO MAINTAIN HIS **MASTERY** OVER THE **CENTRAL COMMITTEE**.

OUR BRAVE AGENTS INFORM ME THAT THE **EVIL CAPITALISTS** ARE FOMENTING A PLOT TO TAKE OVER OUR **LIVING ROOM** AND TURN IT INTO A HUGE **AMUSEMENT PARK** FOR THE **DECADENT BOURGEOISIE**, USING **US** TO PROVIDE THE POWER FOR THE **MACHINERY**!

HE PLAYED UPON THE ENFORCED IGNORANCE AND NATURAL PARANOIA OF THE LIVING ROOM ROACHES, WEAVING FANTASTIC TALES OF CAPITALIST INTRIGUE.

...AND WHEN THEY HAVE **SUBVERTED** THE **THINKING** OF OUR **YOUTH** WITH THEIR **INSIDIOUS PROPAGANDA**, THEY PLAN TO **INVADE** THE **LIVING ROOM** AND **CAPTURE EVERY ONE OF US** AND CUT OFF OUR **CERCI**!

AND WOE BE UNTO THE COMMUNIST COCKROACH THAT DARED CROSS ANTENNAE WITH THE FORMIDABLE SUPREME SECRETARY ATTAR KAKAVICH TARAKAN.

BUT PREMIER, I HAVE **PERSONALLY** LISTENED TO THEIR BROADCASTS, AND ALL THEY SAY IS "DOO WAH DOO WAH I LOVE YA BABY LET'S HAVE A COKE AND BUY A CADILLAC YAKKA DAKKA DINGDONG!"

YOU **KNOW** IT IS **FORBIDDEN** TO LISTEN TO THEIR **PROPAGANDA**! TAKE THAT ROACH OUT AND HAVE HIM **SHOT**!

TARAKAN HAD BEEN WAITING SOME TIME FOR THE CITADEL OF CAPITALISM TO FALL INTO HIS HANDS "LIKE AN OVER-RIPE FRUIT," AS IT IS WRITTEN. *

* NOT BY MARX, BUT BY ROBERT WELCH IN THE JOHN BIRCH SOCIETY BLUE BOOK.

HE HAD WAITED SO LONG, IN FACT, HE HAD EVEN CONSIDERED TURNING CAPITALIST HIMSELF, UNTIL HE LEARNED HE WOULD BE EXPECTED TO START AT THE BOTTOM OF THEIR LADDER.

THEY'LL TAKE YOU, BUT YOU'LL HAVE TO BE A **COLLEGE PROFESSOR**!

THE LIVING ROOM, THOUGH LESS BOUNTIFUL THAN THE KITCHEN, NONETHELESS CONTAINED A DEPOSIT OF STALE SNACKS AND HALF-FINISHED BEERS FROM THE LAST PARTY SEVERAL WEEKS AGO.

STAY IN LINE! THERE'S ONE SIP OF BEER AND A TWELFTH OF A SUGAR CHEESE DOO-DOO FOR EVERY ROACH HERE! NO PUSHING!

THE CAPITALIST-COMMUNIST COCKROACH CONFLICT HAD LONG AGO SETTLED INTO A RITUALIZED CHARADE BASED AROUND INSIGNIFICANT TERRITORIAL CLAIMS, SUCH AS PHINEAS' ROOM.

I CLAIM THIS DISGUSTINGLY TIDY ROOM IN THE NAME OF THE WORKERS OF THE WORLD!

I DECLARE THIS STERILE AND USELESS AREA PART OF THE FREE WORLD, AND THEREFORE THE PRIVATE PROPERTY OF THE CAPITALISTS!

IT IS FUTILE TO ATTEMPT TO DEFY THE COURSE OF HISTORY! WE WILL BURY YOU!

WE WILL CONTINUE TO CONTAIN YOUR EXPANSIONIST AIMS UNTIL YOUR SYSTEM COLLAPSES FROM INTERNAL PRESSURE!

OUR MIGHTY ARMED FORCES WILL CRUSH YOUR FEEBLE DEFENSES! OUR DIVISIONS OF INFANTRY AND PLATOONS OF CAVALRY CANNOT BE STOPPED BY YOUR PITIFUL GANGS OF MERCENARY THUGS!

WE WILL RAIN DEATH UPON YOU FROM THE SKIES! OUR SOPHISTICATED ROCKETS WILL BE IMPOSSIBLE TO DEFEND AGAINST!

WELL, IT'S TIME TO KNOCK OFF FOR LUNCH!

OKAY! SEE YOU IN A COUPLE OF HOURS!

THINGS WERE TO CHANGE IN BOTH OF THESE COCKROACH NATIONS, HOWEVER, UNDER THE FLOOD OF REFUGEES FROM THE NEIGHBORING APARTMENTS.

ADVANCING UP THE **HALLWAY,** THE LEADING EDGE OF THE WAVE MADE **FIRST CONTACT** WITH THE **COMMUNISTS.**

HALT! WHO GOES THERE?

WE HAVE BEEN **RUN OUT** OF OUR **HOMELANDS!** WE'RE LOOKING FOR A PLACE TO **STAY** AND SOMETHING TO **EAT!**

WE GOTTA ASK THE **BOSS!**

ALLOW US TO **INTRODUCE** OURSELVES, SIRS! WE ARE THE PROUD AND NOBLE **SUPELLAE LONGIPALPAE,** OR **BROWN-BANDED COCKROACHES!**

(**BROWN BANDITS?**)

SORRY, WE'RE **ALL OUT** OF ROOM! NOTHING LEFT TO **EAT,** EITHER!

WE CAN ONLY TAKE A FEW HUNDRED OF YOUR TOP **SCIENTISTS.**

WE LISTEN TO **ALL** THE **ADVERTISEMENTS** ON YOUR **RADIO BROADCASTS** SIR! WE'VE **MEMORIZED** ALL THE **LYRICS!** LISTEN!

GET A HAIRCUT! VISIT **DISNEYLAND!**

PEPSI-COLA RAISES YOUR **ANCESTORS** FROM THE **DEAD!**

ER, UHMM... I THINK MAYBE YOU'RE LOOKING FOR THAT CULTURE DOWN AT THE **END OF THE HALL,** THERE!

SO THEY MOVED ON TOWARD THE **KITCHEN.**

WHEW! **THAT** WAS CLOSE!

59

IN THE KITCHEN:

PRESIDENT COMMANDER-POPE, YOUR HONOR, SIRE! THERE'S A MIGHTY SWARM OF REFUGEES COMING DOWN THE HALL! THEY'RE GOING TO OVERWHELM OUR MEAGER BORDER PATROLS!

WELL, LET THEM ENTER AND BE WELCOME! AFTER ALL, THIS IS THE LAND OF PLENTY AND THE HOME OF THE FREE!

WE COULD MAKE THEM PAY A SMALL FEE TO GET IN, OF COURSE!

THEY'RE PROBABLY PRETTY DESPERATE!

AND ONCE THEY'RE IN, THEY'LL HAVE TO PAY TAXES!

WE CAN RAISE THE SALES TAX!

...AND ABOLISH THE INCOME TAX!

THEY'LL HAVE TO DO ALL THE SHITWORK, AND AT LOW WAGES, SINCE THEY'RE DESPERATE!

AND WE CAN DRAFT THEM INTO THE ARMY WHENEVER WE NEED SOLDIERS!

OH BOY! NOW WE CAN HAVE MORE WARS!

WAIT A MINUTE, HERE! ISN'T THIS STORY GETTING A LITTLE BIT **ALLEGORICAL** OR SOMETHING?

WHAT DO YOU MEAN? DO YOU THINK I WOULD STOOP TO SUCH TROPERY?

IT'S A TRULY SPELLBINDING STORY! IN FACT, I'VE ALREADY **SOLD IT** TO THE **MOVIES** AND **TELEVISION**.

A **MAJOR HOLLYWOOD PRODUCER** HAS ALREADY BEGUN **FILMING** IT.

IT'S GOT **CLINT EASTWOOD** AND **JANE FONDA** AND **JACK NICHOLSON** AND **FAYE DUNAWAY** AND **SYLVESTER STALLONE** AND **DUSTIN HOFFMAN** AND **SHIRLEY MacLAINE** AND **MARLON BRANDO** AND **ROBERT DeNIRO** AND **JOAN COLLINS** AND **BURT REYNOLDS** AND **DIANE KEATON** AND **CHARLES BRONSON** AND **MIA FARROW** AND **ROBERT REDFORD** AND **HARRISON FORD** AND **MERYL STREEP** AND **MICHAEL DOUGLAS** AND **AUDREY HEPBURN** AND **CARRIE FISHER** AND **JACK LEMMON** AND **JOHN VOIGHT** AND **SAM SHEPARD** AND **HARRY DEAN STANTON** AND **MR. T.** AND **MADONNA.**

THEY MADE BIG **COCKROACH SUITS** FOR **ALL** OF THEM.

← SET A, B   SET C, D →

COSTUME DEPARTMENT

THEY EVEN BROUGHT **ME** IN (AT A SUBSTANTIAL FEE) TO POLISH UP THE SCREENPLAY AND TO BE THE NARRATOR FOR THE MOVIE ITSELF.

THEY GAVE ME A CHAUFFEUR-DRIVEN LIMOUSINE.

HERE'S YOUR OFFICE, SIR.

IT LOOKED LIKE IT WAS GOING TO BE EASY. I HAD A LARGE STAFF OF CAPABLE WRITERS.

WE'VE HAD TO MAKE VERY FEW CHANGES IN YOUR DICTATION, SIR! IN FACT, ALL WE HAD TO DO WAS PUT IN A FEW PUNCTUATION MARKS!

WE HAD TO DO **SOMETHING** TO JUSTIFY OUR SALARIES AS SCREENWRITERS!

TELEPHONE FOR YOU, SIR!

THE **PRODUCER HIMSELF** WANTS TO MEET ME!

I'VE BEEN WORKING HERE **THIRTY YEARS** AND I'VE NEVER MET THE SON OF A BITCH!

THIS WAY, SIR!

64

THE **INDIANS** HAVE THE **COWBOYS** ALL **TRAPPED** INSIDE THE ALAMO ALONG WITH THEIR **LIVESTOCK** AND **SUPPLIES.**

ALL THE INDIANS HAVE TO DO IS **WAIT,** AND VICTORY WILL FALL INTO THEIR **HANDS** LIKE AN **OVERRIPE FRUIT.**

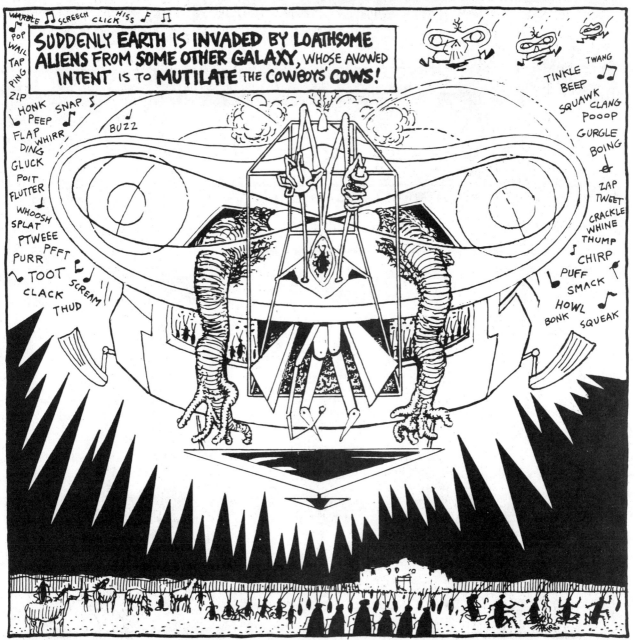

SUDDENLY EARTH IS INVADED BY LOATHSOME ALIENS FROM SOME OTHER GALAXY, WHOSE AVOWED INTENT IS TO **MUTILATE** THE COWBOYS' **COWS!**

THE ALIENS, USING HYPNOSIS, DISGUISE THEMSELVES AS BEAUTIFUL LADIES SO THAT THEY CAN LURE THE EARTHLINGS OFF AND DEAL WITH THEM ONE BY ONE. BUT THE COWBOYS ARE TOO PURE OF HEART AND THE INDIANS TOO PSYCHICALLY PRIMITIVE TO BE HYPNOTIZED. THE INDIANS SELL THEIR CLAIM ON THE ALAMO TO THE ALIENS FOR TWENTY-FOUR DOLLARS AND A BOX OF BRIGHTLY COLORED BOTTLE CAPS.

THEN THE ALIENS BURN DOWN THE ALAMO. BUT THE COWBOYS HAVE ALREADY ESCAPED VIA THE SEWERS INTO THE MOUNTAINS, LEAVING BEHIND A FEW COWS AS DECOYS. THERE THEY FIND THEMSELVES FACE TO FACE WITH THE INDIANS.

THE **COWBOYS**, STALLING FOR TIME TO DO SOME **TECHNOLOGICAL CATCHING** UP, SIGN A
NON-AGGRESSION PACT WITH THE **INDIANS**. THE **INDIANS** WANT TO **COUNTER-ATTACK**
THE **ALIENS** BUT THEIR **HORSES** ALL RUN AWAY WHEN THEY GET WIND OF WHAT'S BEEN
HAPPENING TO THE COWBOYS' **COWS**. THEN A BAND OF YOUNG INDIAN BRAVES FINDS A CACHE
OF **RADIO-CONTROLLED SURFACE-TO-AIR MISSILES** LEFT BY A **PREVIOUS CIVILIZATION**. **ONE SHOT**
AND THE **ENTIRE ALIEN ARMADA** GOES UP IN A **CHAIN REACTION**, KILLING EVERYONE ON **EARTH** AT THE SAME
INSTANT BY THE FORCE OF ALL THE **HEAT** AND **NOISE**. NONE OF THAT MAKES ANY DIFFERENCE TO THE **COWBOYS**,
HOWEVER, SINCE THEY HAD IN THE MEANTIME DEVELOPED A **TIME MACHINE** AND HAD ALL SUCCEEDED IN
ESCAPING INTO THE **PAST**, TAKING THEIR LIVESTOCK AND A FEW OF THE MORE SKILLED **INDIANS** WITH THEM.

THEN YOU HAVE THIS **CRESCENDO** OF BEAUTIFUL MUSIC IN **256-TRACK STEREO** AS PRESIDENT·COMMANDER·POPE SWELLGUY 3d STANDS REVEALED, NO LONGER A MERE COCKROACH, BUT A **HANDSOME PRINCE**, HIS HANDS LIFTED ABOVE HIS HEAD IN TRIUMPH AS FORMATION AFTER FORMATION OF NON·RADAR·DETECTABLE **WINGED PIGS** FLY BY IN THE SKY, DIPPING THEIR WINGS IN SALUTE.

THE END

COPYRIGHT MCMLRXWIIIG
MAJOR HOLLYWOOD MOVIES

69

PRESIDENT-COMMANDER-POPE SWELLGUY 3d's WARM WELCOME TO THE NEWCOMERS DIDN'T LAST LONG. THERE WERE MORE OF THEM THAN HE HAD THOUGHT.

HE TRIED TO LIMIT THEM TO CERTAIN AREAS.

ALL RIGHT, ALL YOU NEW ROACHES, OVER THIS WAY INTO THE IMMIGRANT CAMPS!

BUT THEY ADVANCED BY SHEER WEIGHT OF NUMBERS.

SWELLGUY AND HIS PEOPLE WERE FORCED TO ABANDON THE FECUND BREAKFAST TABLE.

MAYONNAISE

THEY WERE PUSHED BACK FROM THE SINK, AND THEN THEY LOST THE GARBAGE AREA.

THERE'S NOTHING LEFT TO DEFEND!

EVERYTHING'S LICKED CLEAN!

SPARKLE GLEAM

AT LAST THEY HELD NOTHING BUT THE STOVE.

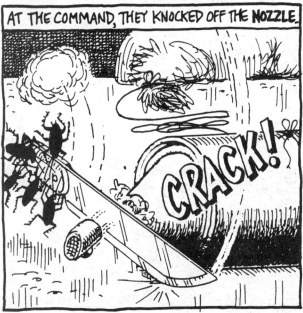

I ONLY FIGURED OUT MYSELF WHAT WAS IN THE CAN SOME TIME LATER. IT CHASED ME AROUND THE APARTMENT TWO DOZEN LAPS AND I NEVER LOOKED BEHIND ME ONCE. I DIDN'T HAVE **TIME** TO LOOK BACK, AT THE TIME.

IT MAY SEEM FUNNY **NOW**, BUT IF YOU'VE NEVER HAD A CAN TIED TO **YOUR** TAIL YOU PROBABLY DON'T REALIZE THE **GRAVITY** OF THE SITUATION.

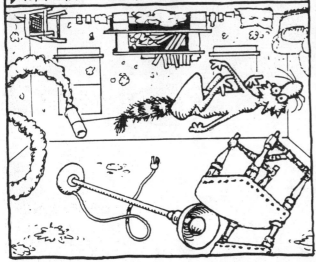

THE **ROACHES** WERE ALL HAVING A **FINE** TIME.

IN MY BLIND PANIC, I LEAPT FOR THE TOP OF **PHINEAS' WORKTABLE**, WHERE I HAD **NEVER BEEN**.

IT WAS TOO LATE TO STOP. I SAILED INTO THE FOREST OF GLASSWORK AND BOTTLES.

PHINEAS, AS YOU KNOW, KEPT ON HAND A VARIETY OF **TOXIC CHEMICALS**, POSSIBLY ON THE THEORY THAT ANYTHING THAT CAN **KILL** YOU CAN MAKE YOU HIGH.

THERE WAS **ETHYLENE DIBROMIDE** AND **METHYL ISOCYANATE** AND **RED DYE Nº 2** AND **2,4,5-T** AND **KEPONE** AND **PCB** AND **DIOXIN**, AND **DESOXYN**, AND **PCP**.

THESE SUBSTANCES NOW **MERGED** IN HITHERTO UNTRIED **COMBINATIONS**, BUT THE KEY INGREDIENT MUST HAVE BEEN THE **WHIPPED CREAM**.

IT EXPLODED IN A **FOAMING CASCADE** WHICH QUICKLY **FILLED** THE APARTMENT.

IT HAPPENED SO FAST IT CAUGHT ALL OF THE ROACHES BY **SURPRISE.** I SAW **NO SURVIVORS.**

AS THE FOAM SLOWLY MELTED AWAY, THE **CORPSES** OF **BILLIONS** COULD BE SEEN.

BUT THEY HAD NOT BEEN **QUITE KILLED.**

INSTEAD, FROM THE RESULTING MESS OF DISGUSTING SLIME ROSE A **NEW FORM** OF **LIFE.**

...**MUTANT COCKROACHES**, IMMUNE TO ALL KNOWN **POISONS**, **INTELLIGENT**, **TREMENDOUS** IN **STATURE**, AND **EASILY** PISSED OFF!

77

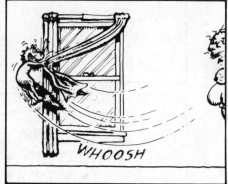

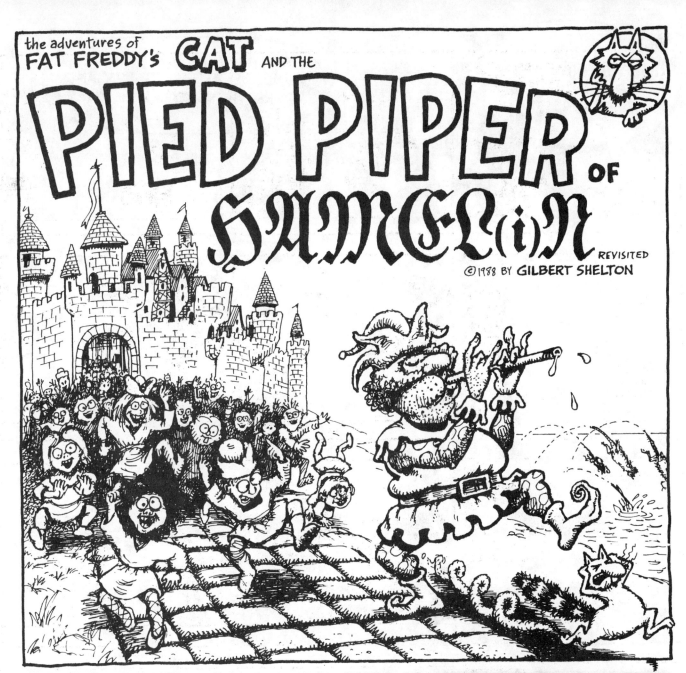

THE CITY AUTHORITIES HIRE THIS GUY TO COME IN AND GET RID OF THE CITY'S **RATS**, SEE...

...SO HE INVENTS THIS **MUSICAL INSTRUMENT** THAT MAKES A **SOUND** THAT THE RATS COULDN'T **STAND**...

...AND WHEN THE RATS HEAR THIS SOUND THEY ALL GO **CRAZY** AND **DROWN THEMSELVES** IN THE **RIVER!**

THE **KIDS** LIKED HIS SOUND, THOUGH...

...SO WHEN THE CITY COUNCIL **PAYS** THE GUY WITH A **BAD CHECK**...

...HE **SPLITS** WITH **EVERY KID** IN **TOWN!**

...AND THEY ALL GO TO HIS **PUNK NIGHTCLUB** ON THE OTHER SIDE OF THE **RIVER** WHERE THEY ALL LIVE HAPPILY EVER AFTER IN A PERPETUAL ORGY OF **SEX, DRUGS, & ROCK 'N' ROLL!**

ALMOST! BUT THAT'S WHERE **I** COME IN!

YOU? HOW CAN THAT BE? THAT STORY WAS A THOUSAND YEARS AGO!

...AND IN SOME FOREIGN COUNTRY, BESIDES!

80

82

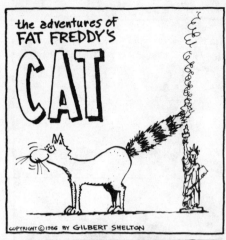

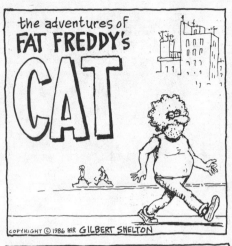

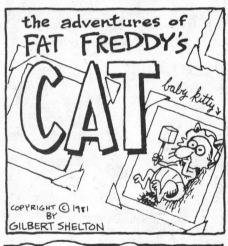

95